Endorsements for the Church Questions Series

"Christians are pressed by very real questions. How does Scripture structure a church, order worship, organize ministry, and define biblical leadership? Those are just examples of the questions that are answered clearly, carefully, and winsomely in this new series from 9Marks. I am so thankful for this ministry and for its incredibly healthy and hopeful influence in so many faithful churches. I eagerly commend this series."

R. Albert Mohler Jr., President, The Southern Baptist Theological Seminary

"Sincere questions deserve thoughtful answers. If you're not sure where to start in answering these questions, let this series serve as a diving board into the pool. These minibooks are winsomely to-the-point and great to read together with one friend or one hundred friends."

Gloria Furman, author, *Missional Motherhood* and *The Pastor's Wife*

T0327147

"As a pastor, I get asked lots of questions. I'm approached by unbelievers seeking to understand the gospel, new believers unsure about next steps, and maturing believers wanting help answering questions from their Christian family, friends, neighbors, or coworkers. It's in these moments that I wish I had a book to give them that was brief, answered their questions, and pointed them in the right direction for further study. Church Questions is a series that provides just that. Each booklet tackles one question in a biblical, brief, and practical manner. The series may be called Church Questions, but it could be called 'Church Answers.' I intend to pick these up by the dozens and give them away regularly. You should too."

Juan R. Sanchez, Senior Pastor, High Pointe Baptist Church, Austin, Texas

"Where can we Christians find reliable answers to our common questions about life together at church—without having to plow through long, expensive books? The Church Questions booklets meet our need with answers that are biblical, thoughtful, and practical. For pastors, this series will prove a trustworthy resource for guiding church members toward deeper wisdom and stronger unity."

Ray Ortlund, President, Renewal Ministries

Does It Matter What I Believe?

Church Questions

Am I Called to Ministry?, Brad Wheeler

Can Women Be Pastors?, Greg Gilbert

Does God Love Everyone?, Matt McCullough

Does It Matter What I Believe?, Samuel James

Does the Gospel Promise Health and Prosperity?, Sean DeMars

How Can I Be Sure I'm Saved?, Jeremy Pierre

How Can I Find Someone to Disciple Me?, Garret Kell

How Can I Get More Out of My Bible Reading?, Jeremy Kimble

How Can I Love Church Members with Different Politics?, Jonathan Leeman and Andy Naselli

How Can I Serve My Church?, Matthew Emadi

How Can I Support International Missions?, Mark Collins

How Can Our Church Find a Faithful Pastor?, Mark Dever

How Can Women Thrive in the Local Church?, Keri Folmar

Is God Really Sovereign?, Conrad Mbewe

Is Hell Real?, Dane Ortlund

Is It Loving to Practice Church Discipline?, Jonathan Leeman

What Do Deacons Do?, Juan Sanchez

What If I Don't Desire to Pray?, John Onwuchekwa

What If I Don't Feel Like Going to Church?, Gunner Gundersen

What If I'm Discouraged in My Evangelism?, Isaac Adams

What Is the Church's Mission?, Jonathan Leeman

What Should I Do Now That I'm a Christian?, Sam Emadi

What Should I Look for in a Church?, Alex Duke

What Should We Do about Members Who Won't Attend?, Alex Duke

Who's in Charge of the Church?, Sam Emadi

Why Is the Lord's Supper So Important?, Aubrey Sequeira

Why Should I Be Baptized?, Bobby Jamieson

Why Should I Give to My Church?, Jamie Dunlop

Why Should I Join a Church?, Mark Dever

Does It Matter What I Believe?

Samuel James

CROSSWAY®

WHEATON, ILLINOIS

Cover image and design: Jordan Singer

First printing 2023

Printed in the United States of America

Trade paperback ISBN: 978-1-4335-7912-7
ePub ISBN: 978-1-4335-7915-8
PDF ISBN: 978-1-4335-7913-4
Mobipocket ISBN: 978-1-4335-7914-1

Library of Congress Cataloging-in-Publication Data

Names: James, Samuel, 1988- author.
Title: Does it matter what I believe? / Samuel James.
Description: Wheaton, Illinois : Crossway, 2022. | Series: Church questions | Includes index.
Identifiers: LCCN 2022023047 (print) | LCCN 2022023048 (ebook) | ISBN 9781433579127 (trade paperback) | ISBN 9781433579134 (pdf) | ISBN 9781433579134 (mobi) | ISBN 9781433579158 (epub)
Subjects: LCSH: Theology.
Classification: LCC BR118 .J36 2022 (print) | LCC BR118 (ebook) | DDC 230—dc23/eng/20220907
LC record available at https://lccn.loc.gov/2022023047
LC ebook record available at https://lccn.loc.gov/2022023048

Crossway is a publishing ministry of Good News Publishers.

BP		32	31	30	29	28	27	26	25	24	23
15	14	13	12	11	10	9	8	7	6	5	4	3	2	1

The law of the LORD is perfect,
    reviving the soul;
the testimony of the LORD is sure,
    making wise the simple;
the precepts of the LORD are right,
    rejoicing the heart;
the commandment of the LORD is pure,
    enlightening the eyes;
the fear of the LORD is clean,
    enduring forever;
the rules of the LORD are true,
    and righteous altogether.

Psalm 19:7–9

Over the past few years, millions of people have tuned in to a Netflix show about cleaning up. *Tidying Up* has become a massive hit, and its Japanese star Marie Kondo has ascended to the heights of influencer culture. In addition to a feverishly popular Netflix program, Kondo now boasts a bestselling book, a highly sought-after online course, and a huge social media following of millions. What's all the rage?

The secret to Kondo's fame is her "KonMari" method, which is all about organizing one's possessions and getting rid of lots of stuff. Kondo's exhortation to those who feel overwhelmed by clutter is simple: Get rid of anything that does not "spark joy." For Kondo, this is not a flippant or casual standard. Over the course of her show, she urges her clients to be ruthless in only keeping what actively provides happiness. Beloved but unworn clothes must be tossed. Books should only be kept to a strict minimum. Sentimental items? Only keep whatever provokes the strongest continual emotional reaction. Everything else needs to go, everything that does not "spark joy."

It's not hard to imagine why such a message might be appealing to many who feel messy or disorganized. Thousands of people have found Kondo's message liberating. Who among us does not need the occasional reminder that material possessions should serve a greater good than mere existence? Down with clutter!

What's fascinating (and saddening) is that there seem to be many Christians, particularly in the affluent West, who think of theology, or doctrine, the way Marie Kondo thinks of clutter. It's not uncommon to hear people in the church talk about the discipline of theology like a pair of shoes or stack of paperbacks taking up too much room. "It's just not helpful," they say, "to talk about election, or justification, or the inerrancy of Scripture. Sure, these things might be good for preachers or scholars to think about, but they just cause arguments among everyone else." This attitude is reflected many places, like sermons that spend two minutes talking about a passage of Scripture and twenty minutes about finances, marriage, or self-esteem or like small group Bible studies where hard questions about Scripture are quickly brushed aside in favor of asking everyone present, "What does this verse mean *to you*?"

To be sure, it's pretty rare for someone in a church to actually come out and say that talking about or studying theology is bad (though this does happen!). What seems to be the case is not that many American Christians actively think of doctrine as bad or harmful but that many believe it is unnecessary. In other words, for many evangelicals, biblical doctrine—the teaching of all Scripture in its fullness, beyond the bare essentials for salvation—is not like poison but like clutter. There's nothing inherently wrong with it, but it does not "spark joy."

And what do we do with things that don't spark joy?

"Doctrine Divides, Jesus Unites" . . . Really?

Many evangelicals are leery of thinking or talking about doctrine, but it's not because of a prejudice against the Bible or Bible teachers. Rather, it can be a conclusion that they reach after watching bitter disputes over Scripture divide, alienate, and wound real people. Many Christians have seen this happen, and it is indeed a heartbreaking sight. One of my best friends is only a couple years into his first pastorate and has already been on the receiving end of angry accusations due to disagreements over doctrine. My father has been in ministry for almost thirty years; believe me, we pastors' kids are not spared the spectacles of church splits, broken friendships, and heartache for the sake of the word. Sometimes the disputes were over massive questions—*Is Jesus really the only way to be saved?*—and sometimes they were over less important issues—*When will Jesus return?* or *What songs should be sung in church?* The point is, these disagreements among believers can wreak astonishing damage in individuals and churches.

Because of this damage, many Christians have arrived at a seductively simple mantra: "Doctrine divides, but Jesus unites." Whether this is spoken out loud or just implied, the idea is the same: theology is controversial and therefore divisive. In order to keep people from being wounded by these disagreements—and perhaps choosing to leave the church—we need to talk less about the difficult or complex teachings of the Bible and stick to the things that we all can agree on.

"Doctrine divides, Jesus unites" usually has two meanings. The first meaning is simply that controversial or emotionally difficult teaching should be avoided. The second meaning is that people are often encouraged to join churches or take on leadership roles *regardless of what they believe.* In this scenario, the question of what people believe about biblical doctrine is mostly irrelevant; what really matters is how nice and friendly they are, how willing they are to serve, or how well put together they make themselves or the church look.

What makes "doctrine divides, Jesus unites" so alluring is not just that it's a catchy slogan but that in many cases it really does seem to hold up as true. To stop caring about what you or other people believe is to open up (at least for a time) a world of possibilities in terms of friendships, partnerships, memberships, and even identity. Relegating core beliefs about God, Scripture, Jesus, and humanity to the margins is often something done for the sake of efficiency, which is why Christians, churches, and organizations that see their mission in primarily economic terms (*How much am I doing? How much are we giving? How big is our bottom line?*) almost invariably drift away from their foundational convictions.

But there are at least two fundamental problems with this idea. The first problem is that it's not true. "Doctrine divides, Jesus unites" is itself a doctrine, a theological statement that says something about Christianity. What it says is incorrect according to Scripture, experience, and reason.

The second problem with this statement is that nobody actually believes it. This might sound strange; haven't I already explained that there are indeed people who believe that doctrine divides because they've seen such division happen? Yes, that's certainly true. But the idea that what you believe about the Bible doesn't really matter is something that none of us can truly think with all our hearts because in other places of our lives we consistently demonstrate that we actually *do* think our beliefs matter. Those who say that doctrine divides and Jesus unites still know that beliefs matter, but they've been convinced to see Christianity as a different kind of belief than other beliefs.

The truth is that we know that what we believe matters. Our instincts may downplay the importance of doctrine, but how often do we turn around and fill up our Facebook and Twitter profiles with all kinds of beliefs about politics, news, etc.? Indeed, many of the people who put up the fiercest resistance against holding Christians accountable to orthodoxy simultaneously talk about their political or social convictions with all the passion of a lifelong theologian.

Our behavior in other areas of life betrays that it matters what we and others believe. So the question is not really, "Do our beliefs matter?" but, "*Which* beliefs matter?"

Doctrine vs. Pragmatism

It's tempting to act as if political beliefs matter but theological beliefs do not because it's often easier to see the real-world implications of politics than theology. If someone has what we consider to be an incorrect view on a political candidate or a law, our instincts are often to engage in discussion because the stakes feel greater. If the wrong candidate gets elected, he or she will enact policies that promote injustice or immorality. We can clearly imagine the consequences of wrong political views on our communities and that motivates our desire to speak up, vote, and take a stand.

By contrast, many people think of doctrine as having little effect on everyday life. Theology seems purely intellectual. While a massive issue such as the divinity of Jesus may seem self-evidently important, topics like the inerrancy of Scripture, the depravity of man, or justification by faith alone can feel remote, theoretical, or even antiquated. How does believing that the book of Job is divinely inspired make you better in your job or marriage? What does it really matter in a world of poverty, hunger, and loneliness if you don't think Jesus is the only way to heaven? Doesn't this world have more pressing problems than trying to "police" people's views on sexuality or gender?

In the life of a Christian and of a church, the absence of doctrine is often the presence of pragmatism. We can struggle to see the relevance of doctrine for everyday life because we measure our everyday lives in terms of efficiency, ease, and minimizing stress. But the Bible calls us to a much richer perspective: it calls us to know the truth. What we believe matters because we were created by a real, triune God who revealed the truth about himself and about us. To not know the truth that our Creator reveals is to be less than fully human.

One person who saw this very clearly was C. S. Lewis. In his essay "Man or Rabbit," Lewis addressed whether a person can live a good life without being a Christian. At the beginning of the essay, Lewis admits that the very question is misleading because it implies that knowing what's really true is separate from a "good" life.

> One of the things that distinguishes man from the other animals is that he wants to know things, wants to find out what reality is like, simply for the sake of knowing. When that desire is completely quenched in anyone, I think he has become something less than human. As a matter of fact,

I don't believe any of you have really lost that desire. More probably, foolish preachers, by always telling you how much Christianity will help you and how good it is for society, have actually led you to forget that Christianity is not a patent medicine. Christianity claims to give an account of facts—to tell you what the real universe is like. Its account of the universe may be true, or it may not, and once the question is really before you, then your natural inquisitiveness must make you want to know the answer. If Christianity is untrue, then no honest man will want to believe it, however helpful it might be: if it is true, every honest man will want to believe it, even if it gives him no help at all.[1]

This is crucial to understand. What we believe about God, the Bible, salvation, and our world matters not primarily because it might make us happier or better at what we do but because of God. There are right and wrong answers to the biggest questions in the universe because there is a real God who really is sovereign and really has revealed himself and his truth. We need to know what he has said.

That doesn't mean that we will fully understand every doctrine perfectly, or that every single theological conversation is equally important, or that there will never be room for disagreement or gray areas. God is a perfect speaker, but we are imperfect hearers. Nevertheless, we really can know him and his revealed truth. We really can study his word and his world and think more like him. This is part of why we exist.

Our temptation is to think of doctrine as clutter that needs to be put away if it doesn't spark joy. But this isn't true. Doctrine isn't the clutter that makes the house stuffy, it's the furniture that makes a house a home: the table where we share meals with loved ones, the seats where we tell and hear stories, the warm bed where we sleep safe and sound. We think of doctrine as clutter only because we don't know it well enough. When we truly dive into biblical doctrine, the truths it reveals become precious and necessary.

Doing Theology All of the Time

Nevertheless, we shouldn't imagine that theology, even though valuable, will not or cannot affect our everyday lives. The fact is that every day finds you and me acting out what we believe (perhaps even unconsciously) about biblical doctrine. Theology is not ultimately what studious readers of the Bible do when they're cloistered together for hours of uninterrupted contemplation. Rather, theology lies at the foundation of every part of our lives as human beings made in the image of God. While not all of us are professional theologians, all of us "do" or practice theology.

We do theology when we vote, as our political beliefs are shaped by what we think is best for people, and that belief depends on how we define what is good.

We do theology when we marry. Our choice of a husband or wife reflects what we value in others and in ourselves, as well as what we believe will make us happy. Those are theological beliefs.

We do theology when we spend our money, as Jesus made very clear (Matt. 6:19–21). We do theology when we parent our children. We do theology in how we do our jobs. We do theology in deciding what kind of friends we want, how we use our time, and what sacrifices to make. Perhaps most of all, we do theology in how we endure suffering.

"The doctrines of the word of God were not intended just to lay claim on your brain," writes Paul Tripp, "but also to capture your heart and transform the way you live."[2] As the Psalm says, "Your word is a lamp to my feet, and a light to my path" (Ps. 119:105). Why does it matter what you and I believe? The reason is God's word is light that illuminates the darkness of this broken and unjust world, guides us on the path to everlasting joy and peace, and reminds us even amid the most blinding tears and terrifying shadows that we are not alone. In the glow of biblical doctrine, our souls are warmed.

There's no part of us that can get along "just fine" without biblical doctrine. God knows it, and that's why he gave us his word. Few things could be as comforting as knowing that God has given us exactly what we need to know from him.

But let's get concrete and talk about a few examples. For the rest of this book, I'm going to consider four major doctrines in Scripture and show why they matter.

Why the Doctrine of Scripture Matters

The Glory of Permanent Words

Picture everyday life but without anything permanent.

You wake up in a different bed on Thursday than you did on Tuesday. Your house, in one zip code last weekend, is a few miles elsewhere today. Your morning commute changes every other workday—interstates some days, unfamiliar back roads other days. The people at your job constantly shuffle in and out. One week your cubicle mate is one person, then the next week it changes. Relationships in general shift around you. Things may stabilize for a little bit, but they are sure to change soon. Life has no discernible rhythm, just endless novelty and transition.

Most people would not be able to live like this for long. Nobody wants all new friends every two weeks. There's something life-giving about the same bed each morning, the same faces to wake up to in the same house. Permanence is an anchor, and while anchors are heavy and can be difficult sometimes, they keep us from being lost at sea. Life without permanence is hardly life.[3]

The Bible is that kind of permanent word for us. Why?

The *inspiration* of Scripture is what makes it a gloriously permanent message. The doctrine of inspiration teaches us that the words of the Bible were put there by people who were divinely inspired to write what they wrote. Inspiration does not teach that God merely "dictated" every word of the Bible or mystically caused the human authors to take up their ink and quills. Rather, the doctrine of inspiration tells us that the Holy Spirit moved the writers (2 Pet. 1:21) to record the genuine message of God to his people.

When we say that all Scripture is breathed out by God (2 Tim. 3:16), when we say that the law of the Lord is perfect (Ps. 19:7), and when we say that the word of God is truth itself (John 17:17), we are saying that, at the end of the day, there is one perfectly reliable thing we can hang our lives on day after anxious day. We don't trust the Bible because it's convenient or because we happen to enjoy how it looks in our hands or sounds in our ears. We trust the Bible because it really is a definitive, trustworthy revelation from the actual Creator of the universe.

The inspiration of Scripture matters crucially to us as Christians. Throughout history, some have suggested that only parts of the Bible are actually inspired, while others have said that none of the Bible is "inspired" in this sense, since it is only a human document. But not only does Scripture clearly teach that it is inspired by God (all of it), the doctrine of inspiration is the only hope we have that the God on whose promises we depend is actually the real God of history. The great Anglican theologian J. I. Packer writes, "If the canonical Scriptures were not God's revealed Word, but only a mere fallible human witness to God's Word," no person alive "could be sure that he had a single definite promise from God on which to rest."[4]

Every single day, we are inundated with more words than we can possibly parse. Thousands of articles are published every day online, to go along with hundreds of millions of tweets, millions of hours of audio and video, and innumerable conversations. The modern world is a seemingly infinite whirlpool of talk, a thick and cloudy fog that never seems to let up. The Bible cuts through all of that. The inspired word of God brings all the noise to heel; with authority not of this world, the Bible tells us what we need to know.

While the doctrine of inspiration is certainly counterintuitive in a pluralistic, materialistic society, it matters immeasurably to God's people. Without it, we would be left to ourselves to pick and choose what parts of the Bible sound legit to us and which parts don't. Without inspiration, not only would the moral commands that reveal what's true and right be completely up for grabs, the grace and the mercy that's offered to people who fall short of those commands (everyone!) would be little more than wishful thinking. The doctrine of inspiration is the bedrock foundation of our confidence; even when the storms of doubt and confusion batter us, the foundation is immovable, and we can wait out the storms not in our own strength but on the promises of God's perfect, inspired Word.

Why the Doctrine of God Matters

God Is Trinity . . . Therefore, He Is Good

If you're like me, you may not have thought very much about the Trinity in your Christian life. Most of us who were raised in the church know that there is one God who exists in three persons: Father, Son, and Spirit. We know that Jesus is truly God and truly man, and we know the Spirit is truly God (though many don't know much else about him). For many of us, though, these are simply the details we were taught to believe about Christianity. We don't often ask what difference it makes whether God is just one person or three or whether the Spirit is fully God or whether the Trinity is like a three-leaf clover, the three phases of water, or something else entirely.

We don't know why the Trinity matters. But it does!

Once in a theology class, the professor asked, "Do Jews and Christians worship the same God?" Several students, including myself, answered yes. But that was because we were thinking of God incorrectly. As the professor explained, Christians believe that God exists as Trinity, whereas Jews, Muslims, and the vast majority of the world's theistic religions believe that god only can exist as one.[5] God's being Trinity is not a minor detail; it's a fundamental aspect of his nature, the most essential thing we can know and say and worship about him. God does not perform the Trinity, nor does he merely appear in some ways like a Trinity. God is a Trinity. A god who is not a Trinity is not the God of the Bible.

In his stunning book *Delighting in the Trinity*, theologian Michael Reeves lays out in beautiful detail why God's Trinitarian nature defines and transforms everything we know about God. In sum, God's eternal nature as Father, Son, and Spirit reveals that God's innermost being is an awesome, life-generating love that spills over and refills himself continually. The Trinity makes creation, salvation, and sanctification possible because creation, salvation, and sanctification flow directly out of God's nature as Trinity.

To know God is to know Father, Son, and Spirit as three persons in one essence. There is no other god to know, and there is no other god who saves.

God Is Creator . . . Therefore, His Works Are Good

God is Trinity, and out of the eternal abundance of his triune life and goodness, he creates everything. It is therefore not surprising that God looks at his creation and declares it very good (Gen. 1:31), nor is it surprising that God's people have constantly found in God's created world a beauty and wonder that draws them in gratitude toward him (Ps. 8; 24:1–2).

Why does it matter that God is Creator? There are many reasons but two in particular stand out.

First, many religions teach that the secret to eternal life and happiness is to try to escape the physical world. Buddhism, one of the largest religions in the world, offers followers a psychological and emotional paradise that is totally disembodied. For the Buddhist, eternal life means becoming one with the universe, casting off physical existence, which is itself an evil hindrance to blessing.

That God is Creator means the physical world is not inherently evil. A triune God, who is himself goodness, cannot create an intrinsically evil world. The fallenness of our universe—the tendency in all created things toward death and decay—is a result of human sin, not evil of the material world (Rom. 5:12). Further, the eternal Son of God was incarnated in a physical body so that he could live the life every human is obligated to live, die the death every human is doomed to die, and come to life again to offer forgiveness of sin and the hope of life in a glorified body within a totally renewed earth (Revelation 21). Because God is Creator, we know that he loves and cares for what he has made and that our bodies and our earth are good gifts that groan under the curse of sin but await final redemption through the work of Jesus (Rom. 8:22–23).

Second, God's role as Creator matters because of the authority such a position naturally gives to God. Ours is an age that is extremely suspicious (and often hostile) toward the idea of divine authority. From politics to pop culture, the Western world in particular cherishes the right of any individual to self-determination. Crucial to self-determination is the idea that nobody "owns" any of us in an authoritative sense, which is why traditional belief in a God who designed us and has a rightful claim to our loyalty has declined in recent decades.

The Bible is clear, though, that God's creation of us establishes a Creator-creature relationship between God and man. To deny God's identity as Creator is to declare rebellious independence from him. Such independence, however, does not result in our true freedom and happiness. Apart from creaturely worship and submission to God, we experience only burnout, disappointment, and the existential crises that come from having to create our own meaning. The writers of the 1563 Heidelberg Catechism knew that our belonging to God was the best news possible:

Q. What is your only comfort in life and in death?

A. That I am not my own, but belong—body and soul, in life and in death—to my faithful Savior, Jesus Christ.

Because God is the Creator, we belong to him, and because we belong to him, we have an unshakeable comfort in life and death.

God Is Sovereign . . . Therefore,
His Plans Are Good

Of all the biblical doctrines that Christians may suspect do not "spark joy," the doctrine of God's sovereignty may be near the top of the list. This indeed can be a difficult truth to wrestle with. We stumble over how God can be fully sovereign and yet humans can still be responsible; our heads spin when we try to grasp how God can completely control every moment of human history and yet not be the author of sin. These are deep waters, but we do well to dive in.

Unfortunately, this is not the space to sufficiently unpack all of these deep questions. For now, we will simply observe that the Bible teaches both that God is the omnipotent sovereign over all of creation and all of history and that human beings have real moral agency, can make real decisions, and will be held accountable to God on the last day (where all of human sin, carried out under the providence of God, will ultimately fall either on the sinner or on Jesus Christ on that sinner's behalf).

But . . . does all of that really matter?

We could go over hundreds of ways that believing in God's good sovereignty transforms your life. But perhaps the most direct way is in suffering.

In a fallen world, suffering, sin, and death often feel overwhelming. Cancer and chronic illness take away loved ones, even children. Relationships are torn apart; dreams are crushed, hopes fail, and even the best this life can provide never endures.

To say that God is sovereign—to say that he is totally in control of everything that happens, that nothing in this universe occurs without his express authority—is to say that suffering is not the last word. A God who is surprised or unsure about the bad things that happen to his people cannot guarantee that "For those who love God all things work together for good" (Rom. 8:28). A God who cannot unfailingly choose to save those he elects also cannot promise to bring to completion the good work he starts in us (Phil. 1:6). All of the truths about God that give us rest in our uncertain, sin-entangled, suffering existences flow out of the truth that God is sovereign.

We are tempted to minimize or avoid the doctrine of God's sovereignty because we cannot fully understand it. But a God we can fully understand would hardly be a God worth worshiping! It is enough to receive what God says in his word about his sovereignty and our responsibility; we don't have to master the synthesis between these two realities. If we receive Scripture in its fullness, we will have more than enough to rest our spirits on. We will work out our own salvation each day, knowing that ultimately it is God who works in us (Phil. 2:12–13).

Why the Doctrine of Salvation Matters

Recently, I came across a fascinating statistic.

Even with the increase of the religious "nones" and the decline in churchgoing in America, a whopping 73 percent of Americans believe in heaven. But only 62 percent believe in hell.

I have to admit that I have a lot of sympathy for the people represented in that 11 percent gap. Who wouldn't sell all they had to live in a world of just heaven, no hell? Truly this is one of the most difficult, counterintuitive, and controversial teachings of the Bible. To stand up in any group of modern, Western people and say that the only way to experience eternal life is to trust Jesus Christ is to announce yourself as a backward, bigoted person. Sure, Christianity might work for you, but surely people who are genuinely convinced otherwise but still good people don't deserve hell?

Given our pluralistic, pragmatic culture in the West today, we can find ourselves tempted to take shortcuts with the doctrine of salvation. But this is a devastating mistake for two reasons. First, the Bible couldn't be clearer that there is only one name under heaven by which humans can be saved, and that apart from him, there is only judgment and death. Second, Jesus's sufficient atonement for our sins and resurrection from the dead is the only truth that really meets the needs of our world. To downplay or tinker with these realities does not help anyone; it's giving salt water to a person dying of thirst.

The gospel is the announcement that God— the only Creator and sustainer of the universe— has revealed himself through his Son (Heb. 1:2).

Contrary to what Islam teaches, Jesus was not simply another prophet who taught people what God had told him. Rather, the Bible is absolutely clear that Jesus is God himself, God the Son incarnate, the second person of the eternal Trinity. Because of this fact, what Jesus accomplished on the cross is the definitive work of salvation for sinners. There is no other way to get to God because there is no one else in whom "the whole fullness of deity dwells bodily" (Col. 2:9). Jesus himself said: "I am the way, the truth, and the life. No one comes to the Father except through me" (John 14:6).

People who say that Christians are necessarily "exclusive" and hateful toward others for saying that every other religion is untrue are making the same kind of statement they criticize. To believe that Jesus is not the only way to God is to believe that he is not who he said he was and that the Bible is wrong in what it teaches. Rather than thinking of the doctrine of salvation as a weapon that Christians use to bludgeon unbelievers, we should receive it as an unbelievably glorious revealing of how anyone, anywhere can be saved. The doctrine of salvation is what makes grace free to me and you, regardless of what we've done or where we come from.

Despite the protests of secular culture, nothing but the gospel can really fix what's wrong in us. Only in the gospel do we see a perfect answer to the sin and brokenness that's around us. Only in the gospel do we see the bloody, cancerous, hateful, bigoted, warring, and lost nature of our world called exactly what it is and met with a real solution: not trying harder, not ignoring it, but receiving the grace of the God who became man and took on the curse of sin and death for us. In his broken body, our broken selves become whole. In his shed blood, our corrupted blood becomes clean. In his resurrection, our dead spirits come back to life forever.

The doctrine of salvation is also a reminder that the injustice and evil of this world does not have the final answer. There will be a day where tears are wiped away, hatred and selfishness are banished, and everything is made new

(Rev. 21:1–5). In a world where we are all told every day that the answer to our despair is either to get more stuff or to punish those who disagree with us, what could be more welcome news than the news about a risen Savior who will return to make it all right?

Why the Doctrine of the Church Matters

Let me paint you a scenario.

The alarm on your phone goes off softly. You reach over to turn it off, and you start to hear the pitter-patter of raindrops on the window. As they tap on the glass, you feel the warmth of your pillow all over again and pull the covers up. Nothing sounds better than another few minutes in bed, maybe followed by a hot cup of coffee and an easygoing morning, relaxed on the sofa while the gray clouds sail aimlessly by.

And then the realization breaks on you like a bucket of cold water: It's Sunday. You will have to leave in an hour to make it to church on time. The bed is calling your name.

What do you do?

We tend to think of doctrine as abstract and philosophical. But in this moment, what you believe about the doctrine of the church is going to decide where you spend this sleepy Sunday morning. Does it really make a difference whether you read your Bible on the couch or sit in an uncomfortable pew, surrounded by strangers, while a preacher reads it to you for 30 or 45 minutes?

The answer is: yes! It makes all the difference in the world, and the doctrine of the church is the reason why.

According to the Bible, Jesus's death and resurrection did more than secure the salvation of individual people. It established a community, and this community is not like an ordinary hobby group or country club. This community is a living, embodied picture of the new creation that the risen Jesus is making and will complete when he returns. This community matters so much that the Bible actually calls it Jesus's "bride" and even his own body (1 Cor. 12:13–26; Rev. 19:7). The moment every Christian is saved from sin and raised to spiritual life, he or she becomes part of this body, and membership in this living, breathing community is a fundamental part of a Christian's identity.

This can sound incredibly strange in our culture. Whether we're shopping for a phone, a club, or even a relationship, we often want to hear three words: "No commitment necessary." Sure, belonging to something can be fun, but we want it to be on our schedule and expect it to meet our expectations. The minute it's "just not working" anymore, we want to know we can bail and try something else.

But the Bible teaches us that the church isn't like this. To belong to Christ is to belong to his body. That's why so much of the New Testament talks about the "one another" commands: encourage one another, admonish one another, love one another, honor one another, serve one another. It is impossible for a Christian to faithfully obey these commands alone. By definition, obedience to Scripture requires every Christian to be part of a local church. Just like our arms and legs receive life only when connected to the whole body, our spiritual lives get power and effectiveness only when connected to Jesus's body.

Believing this transforms how you spend your time. Being part of the body requires presence, and often this will mean sacrificing other things for the sake of our brothers and sisters in Christ. But this doesn't just require something from you, it gives something incredibly precious to you. Because of the doctrine of the church, you are never alone in this world. Your battle against temptation, sin, and unbelief are not battles you have to summon the inner strength to fight by yourself. They are battles to be waged alongside fellow soldiers. Your struggle to believe that the gospel really does apply to you, that you really are loved and forgiven and cleansed by Jesus, is not a struggle you have to engage in the solitude of your own head. The Holy Spirit speaks the promises of God's word to you through the lips of others. When everything looks hopeless and lost to you, your Christian brothers and sisters are there to say, "Remember everything that Jesus promised us!"

As we live as members of Jesus's body, we are being shaped by him, through the preaching of his word, through the ordinances of baptism and the Lord's Supper, and through the friendships with our brothers and sisters in Christ. In the local church, all the promises of God in Jesus take a visible, touchable, hearable form, and we get a sneak peek at what our future with our risen Christ looks like. We are not left to ourselves. We have a family, and we have a home that not even death can take away.

These truths are not just ideas to contemplate or argue. They are joys that give life. They are hope that sustains in suffering. They are anchors for the restless soul. When we look into biblical doctrine, we shouldn't ask, "How much of this can I do without?" Instead, we should say, "How could I ever go without this?"

Imagine you met a person who had once been dead but had come back to life. Imagine that this person had raised other dead people to life, had fed thousands of people with only scraps of food, and had healed the blind, the deaf, and the crippled with only a touch. Imagine this person came to you and changed your life forever. What would you do while this person spoke and taught you? You wouldn't try to get by on the bare essentials. You would hang on every word. So would I.

And so we should.

Doctrine Matters

Does it matter what you and I believe? Yes. We know from both Scripture and experience that our beliefs matter. Our lives bear witness that there is truth and there is falsehood, and our souls cry out to know the difference. When we look deeply into biblical teaching, we find more than interesting information. We find objective truth that makes radical claims on us. The doctrine of Scripture anchors our confidence and gives us our spiritual true north. The doctrine of God presents us the only worthy object of our worship. The doctrine of salvation shows us the way out of shame and despair. The doctrine of the church gives us brothers and sisters who help remind us of all this.

Never believe for a second that doctrine divides but Jesus unites. Biblical doctrine is from Jesus, and it only makes us whole. You and I will never regret one minute we spend learning, believing, and obeying the voice of our Savior.

Recommended Resources

Greg Gilbert. *Why Trust the Bible?* Wheaton, IL: Crossway, 2015.

C. S. Lewis. *Mere Christianity*. New York: Harper-Collins, 1952.

Michael Reeves. *Delighting in the Trinity: An Introduction to the Christian Faith*. Downers Grove, IL: InterVarsity Press, 2012.

Paul David Tripp. *Do You Believe? 12 Historic Doctrines to Change Your Everyday Life*. Wheaton, IL: Crossway, 2021.

Notes

1. C. S. Lewis, "Man or Rabbit," in *God in the Dock: Essays on Theology and Ethics* (Grand Rapids, MI: Eerdmans, 1970), 108.

2. Paul Tripp, *Do You Believe? 12 Historic Doctrines to Change Your Everyday Life* (Wheaton, IL: Crossway, 2021), 22.

3. Portions of this section are adapted from my article, "The Glory of Permanent Words," Letter & Liturgy (blog), March 18, 2018, https://letterandliturgy.wordpress.com.

4. J. I. Packer, "The Necessity of the Revealed Word of God," in *Honouring the Written Word of God: Collected Shorter Writings of J. I. Packer*, vol. 3 (Carlisle: Paternoster, 1999), 107–8.

5. Of course, God's revelation of himself throughout Scripture was progressive, which is why the people of God did not explicitly realize God's trinitarian nature at first. Even throughout the Old Testament however there is a pattern of trinitarian language about God. See Scott R. Swain, *The Trinity: An Introduction* (Wheaton, IL: Crossway, 2020).

Scripture Index

Genesis
1:31 29

Psalms
8 30
19:7 25
24:1–2 30
119:105 22

Matthew
6:19–21 22

John
14:6 37
17:17 25

Romans
5:12 30
8:22–23 31
8:28 34

1 Corinthians
12:13–26 40

Philippians
1:6 34
2:12–13 35

Colossians
2:9 37

2 Timothy
3:16 25

Hebrews
1:2 36

2 Peter
1:21 24

Revelation
19:7 40
21 31
21:1–5 38–39

Scripture Index

IX 9Marks

Building Healthy Churches

9Marks exists to equip church leaders with a biblical vision and practical resources for displaying God's glory to the nations through healthy churches.

To that end, we want to see churches characterized by these nine marks of health:

1. Expositional Preaching
2. Gospel Doctrine
3. A Biblical Understanding of Conversion and Evangelism
4. Biblical Church Membership
5. Biblical Church Discipline
6. A Biblical Concern for Discipleship and Growth
7. Biblical Church Leadership
8. A Biblical Understanding of the Practice of Prayer
9. A Biblical Understanding and Practice of Missions

Find all our Crossway titles and other resources at 9Marks.org.

John
Onwuchekwa
Church Questions

Sam
Emadi
Church Questions

Mark
Dever
Church Questions

el Like
Church?

Does
God Love
Everyone?

Matt
McCullough
Church Questions

How Can
I Find Someone
to Disciple Me?

J. Garrett
Kell
Church Questions

How Can
Women T
the Local

Keri
Folmar
Church Questions

zed?

How Can Our
Church Find
a Faithful Pastor?

Mark
Dever
Church Questions

Is It Loving to
Practice Church
Discipline?

Jonathan
Leeman
Church Questions

How Can
I Love Ch
Members
Different

Jonathan
& Andy N
Church Questions

IX 9Marks Church Questions

Providing ordinary Christians with sound and
accessible biblical teaching by answering
common questions about church life.

For more information, visit crossway.org.